Dog Kennel Blues

Poems and Images
from two continents

London College of Communication

Edited by
Tony Wailey &
Susana Sambade

Dog Kennel Blues
Poems and Images from two continents

Published by iKraal
P.O. Box 5326
Kenilworth, 7745
South Africa

First Published 2008

The moral rights of the authors have been asserted

ISBN: 978-0-9585088-2-7

Designed by The Design Practice, London
www.thedesignpractice.net
Printed by Fulmar, London
www.fulmar.com
Published by iKraal, Cape Town
www.ikraal.co.za

Foreword

This publication is based upon an exhibition of poetry and art inspired by socio-political themes from the last three decades of South African history. The linocuts and different artwork are a powerful record of time and place. Beyond the images is a remarkable rhetoric about African identity, expressed in the subjects' style and glimpse of setting. It is a unique reminder of an environment that even now has exemplified the importance of artistic experience in the life of urban, township and rural South Africa and its communities. A substantial number of images are by the celebrated artist/printmaker Billy Mandindi (1967–2005) who played a prominent part in the South African resistance art movement.

The images of striking black-and-white prints, linocuts and other multi-disciplinary work were originally exhibited at LCC in October 2006. This was the first public exhibition of the Hard Ground Printmakers, a group of artists from Cape Town.

The idea for the exhibition developed from a partnership between London College of Communication and Cape Peninsula University of Technology. The initial exhibition in October 2006 marked the start of a project to develop enterprise and innovation in design and the visual arts in both institutions which is being continued through the creative writing series of electives.

In addition, professional writing tutors from the College began working with pupils from Dog Kennel Hill Junior School to produce original poems, based around themes used by the Cape Town artists. The poems and artwork along with poems from Cape Peninsula University are testimony to the way that these relationships have flourished.

Of equal importance is the relationship between text and image that has become one of the main signatures in the developments of creative writing here at the college and has encouraged many new writers into poetry and prose. I would like to thank all the contributors, editors and publishers who helped this book see the light of day but can I particularly thank the Hard Ground Printmakers for continuing to extend that professional link between working practitioners in art design and communication which the college feels is so important for its students.

Special thanks goes to Jonathan Comerford who has helped us with the Group's work, to Ronnie McGrath who worked with the children of Dog Kennel Hill and to Edwine Simon for her work with the students in Cape Town. The College now has an increasingly extensive archive and we are particularly grateful to Jonathan for extending all the exhibited work the Hard Ground has shown here at the LCC. Thank you all. I hope everyone will enjoy this publication.

Marilyn McMenemy
Acting Head of College (2007–2008) LCC
University of the Arts London

Introduction

'We make sense of our own personal identities in much the same way as we do of the identities of characters in stories.' Ricoeur (2000)

Interpreting competing maps, illustrations and signposts for learners is an important part of the methods of teaching and learning across either age or continent. In terms of transitions within that learning this publication focuses upon a group of electives that explore Creative Writing and are offered to all second year students of BA Honours and FdA programmes across the London College of Communication. The students who opt to take these electives are primarily involved in visual or other communication disciplines.

Students wrote original poems exploring the themes and emotions evoked by South African artists – the Hard Ground Printmakers – whose work, depicting life in South Africa over the last two decades, was originally shown at the College in October 2006. In addition professional writers associated with these Creative Writing electives also held workshops in Dog Kennel Hill School over the period of a term with two year five groups. Finally poems were submitted from Cape Peninsula University by students who had a close association with the artists and printmakers who were based in Cape Town and were familiar with the work. Curiously enough they also had links with the LCC and Dog Kennel Hill School. It's a small world.

A Centre for Excellence in Teaching and Learning research grant administered by the University of the Arts London helped to fund the research that informs this publication whilst another from the British Council, awarded to the College for its work in Southern Africa, also contributed to its final production. Many more links with Schools and Southern African universities have been developed over the past year and are the subject of increasingly collaborative pieces of work. This book forms part of a wider dialogue in the relationship between visual and text-based skills within an art, design and communication environment. Its aim is to capture a multi dimensional voice that draws together issues of Creativity, Diversity and Widening Participation across different fields, different ages and different continents.

Overview

Everyone wants to be seen as a person that carries value. It is when we see values in others that our own identity is enhanced. This forms part of a wider debate in the relationships between skills, knowledge and values in both visual and text based worlds. Ivanic has noted that (Hunt & Sampson, 2005) as with all other presentations of self, writers want to be seen as 'valuable' people. It is within this messy 'in between world' that students move to integrate non-formal and formal propositional knowledge, the ability to process a wider view of the world. In other words the ability to comprehend the multiple perspectives that make up everyday life.

This focus concerns identity; the methodology used here aims to capture these perspectives – professional writers, students and junior school children's individual voices. It draws upon the work of Ricoeur (2000) in aiming to allow participants to give an account of their world view and how that is negotiated in the relationship between text and image. Poems in this book focus on this messy in between world of text and image and

of what we are able to achieve in the present moment.
A total of over 500 poems were submitted, of which
135 are represented here. In consideration of space
only one poem was accepted from each author although
many had submitted three poems and in some cases
five. All were subject to the collective editorial knife and
for that, apologies.

If the exhibition exists in the fertile ground of this in
between world then that world itself is an area of
transition. In migration studies it is that of families caught
between home and the far horizon, in the sociology of
cultural writing between the cosmopolitan and the locale,
in economics the Northern and Southern hemispheres.
The graphic concept of Relay notes the interplay
between illustration and writing. The in between world
is always multi-dimensional, capable of many
interpretations. One of the focal points of this exhibition
was to encourage the relationship between text and
image in order to engage with other perspectives.
To explore in other words what Deleuze (2003 ed) refers
to as intertextuality through engaging with other series
of relationships concerning issues of creativity and
diversity between text and image and everything that
comes between.

If this publication is to explore what meanings are held
in those relationships then it is also to enquire what are
the proven features of getting people to write creatively
in the first instance outside of their normal disciplines.
In writing these poems the opportunity to read, see and
write within an interpretative framework appears to have
had a transformative effect on many students. Some
writers talk of causing the reconfiguration of the self
between experience and the text.

For the children of Dog Kennel Hill it was the time before the last year of primary school, before exams and secondary school, between choices, hopes and anxieties. However in that arena of sensation, feeling and learning, all of the students from the three institutions were in some stage of transition.

During this time many felt that the reading and seeing on the course was equally as important in their journey to become creative writers. According to Campbell (Hunt & Sampson, 2005) 'When we read we bring to the literary text our unspoken and experiential life stories. This process of reading between narrative and self reference is also through a language which does not reflect reality but often transfigures it so that meaning and self-understanding go hand in hand with new possibilities of the world in relation to the text.'

The students at the college were asked to write an imaginary account of the skills and knowledge of a professional writer. The answers showed that they believed professional writers were those who 'earn lots of money' and 'always gets paid for work they produce'. They also saw a professional writer as someone who was observant, wrote regularly, was disciplined,imaginative and creative, and had an ability to express their feelings and an incredible capacity to express themselves effectively to their target audience.

Overall the students held a romantic view of what a professional writer's life was like. This had resonances with the Paris of the 1950s and 'drinking lots of coffee', 'phoning and emailing regarding work that they could pick and chose from' or 'doing their work from the comfort of their living rooms'. It was here that skills and knowledge began to merge into perceptions and then values. As the poet Phillip Larkin wrote, 'Thoughts harden into habits'.

Children in the school had a series of lessons with a professional writer working with loose images before going near poetry. Graphic Design students at Cape Town wrote what came out of their hearts. The prints and lithographs and linocuts of the artists were of their home territory.

The majority of the older students wanted to 'explore different types of writing styles' as they were, for example, interested in the various styles of poetry and wanted to learn how 'to write stories instead of just essays'. Others saw writing as being a form of therapy. The research established the feelings professional writers 'wanted to develop in all students' regarding skills, knowledge and values. The central concern was for students to engage with the ability to find their own voice.

Assignment

One of the assignments was to write a short poem or piece of text to accompany images of the black and white prints, linocuts and other multi-disciplinary work exhibited at the 'Impressions' exhibition held at the college during this period. This exhibition by the Hard Ground Printmakers featured black artists, with the curator, Jonathan Comerford, a printer and artist as founder of the project. Many thanks are due to Jonathan for his kind permission to let us use this work. Copyright issues are the bane of any joint publication between text and image. The exhibition complete with poems was shown again in April 2007.

The assignment provided an opportunity and space for all to create a piece of writing with which to: adopt an intuitive approach to writing poetry where they were asked to trust their imagination, take risks, allow room for mistakes, write often and 'voluminously' to provide a palette of colours, of textures and of language (Harper, 2006) by this process students would have a chance of being able to:

- Express themselves;
- Respond to a need or desire;
- React to an experience;
- Make connections between the known and the unknown, the concrete and the abstract, the worldly and the spiritual, among different people, places and cultural backgrounds.

The way in which the assignment was approached could be seen by each participant's particular perspective and social and ethical codes. The variance amongst students in both the way a problem was approached perceived and resolved illustrated a multiplicity of learning experiences and reflected perspectives with age, gender, and colour and more importantly on 'being within the world'.

These findings allowed students to receive constructive criticism from both the professional writers, children and their fellow students. Students were encouraged by the writers to discuss the poem's 'architecture' as they would their main 'visual' subject. During feedback sessions it became apparent that all had interpreted the images in many different ways. The interpretation of the image involved a constant movement between guessing and validating. The students made a guess about the meaning of a part and checked it against the whole and vice versa. Then they guessed the relative importance of the several parts. This 'guessing' with confidence at the wider sum of the parts was one of the constituents' greater sense of creative self expression.

According to Bishop (Earnshaw, 2007) as the process begins to take shape 'Classrooms need to encourage and reward risk taking and experimentation as here you learn to conform but also break genre convention. Here, then is the possibility that composition of formal studies and creative writing are versions of the same field.'

The anthropologist Paul Ricoeur suggests the way a writer affects a reader as 'I speak to someone. I affect someone by the doings and making I either perform or leave undone. Every narrative I construct always involves the intersection of at least two human lives. And every imputation that I make implies at least two persons, one of whom bears some responsibility of someone else's well being.' (Ricoeur, 2000) The writing process pre-supposes a principle of universal translatability despite often being located within a diverse 'in between world'.

The proposition is simple: It is that life is never simple and that understanding some of its complexity brings its own positive rewards in terms of ambiguity, diversity and richness. To reach this point a wide range of processes are required. Those who chose to write poems relied on participation and maximised the work that the ambiguity inherent in this form could inform their negotiation of meaning. Some of the children talked about closing their eyes.

An essential factor was the need for imagination. 'Imagination is an important component of our experience of the world and our sense of place in it.' Here is the world of diversity and transition. For Wenger, people try to align themselves with expectations as an expression of their belonging to the broader social system in which their industry operates. Learning transforms who we are and what we can do and therefore it is an experience of identity (Wenger, 2005). The 'in-between world' consists of a mix of perceiving, interpreting, using, reusing, decoding, and recasting, making, designing, representing, naming, encoding and describing, interacting and forming communal experiences where imagination crosses into identity.

The act of writing a piece to accompany an image suggested that the students were projecting meaning into the world and then perceived this meaning as existing in the world, as if the piece of work produced had a reality of its own. These writers were engaged in negotiating visual disciplines to the word. In the same way a student completes the image so the reader completes the students' written piece. From such a perspective, communication becomes not just a quantitative issue but also a value laden series of negotiations with feeling, seeing writing and learning at their centre.

This world of transition between the formal and the non-formal rests in between these 'values', skills and knowledge. In other words creativity and participation is not something we can just switch on and off like a light bulb but rests within the boundaries of this world where as James Joyce noted 'the ordinary soul turns and whispers'.

Realisation

In *The Poetics of the Open Work*, Umberto Eco suggests that with any image, the number of possible interpretations may have been rationally organized, oriented, and endowed with specification by the artist for its development but the image they produce only gains its aesthetic validity precisely in proportion to the number of different perspectives from which it can be viewed and understood (Eco 2005). Beside the exhibition of images and poems shown at the College in April and May, the event was also constructed in the virtual learning environment of Second Life, where visitors have continued to visit from all over the world. One physical presence noted that 'The poems change the way you view the print because each poet has interpreted the print in a particular way' another added, 'When you come back the following week you see something different'.

Students expressed the feeling that they had 'become increasingly aware of how their own and other's decision-making effected written work and image making'. The writing process is situated within this interactive dynamic mechanism. Feedback at the exhibition demonstrated the same effect in relationships both within and between disciplines. Regardless of whether or not they had been awarded a prize most exhibiting students generally felt more confident about their writing and enthusiastic about continuing to write. They saw their work being exhibited as a first official step in being validated as brothers and sisters of the pen.

According to a number of publications concerning Inspiration 'there is a writing "I" and a writer "I" who, through writing comes to understand what the writing

"I" was doing all along. Sometimes the writer "I"
only emerges at the time when writing occurs, and
that calling up this writer "I" can be a surprise to the
everyday – "I". This sometimes explains why students
felt "strange" about seeing their work as if they were
seeing their writer "I" for the first time' (Earnshaw 2007).
Within this in between world the children just laughed
and wanted to see their work up on the wall next to the
images, to show their parents and their friends and to
enjoy a night out full of laughter and music, prizes, jugs
of juice and packets of crisps.

The overall experience of the contributors, despite their
ages and their relationship to life, text and Image
could be summarised by the great French philosopher
Maurice Merleau-Ponty: 'Tomorrow, with more
experience and insight, I shall possibly understand
it differently. My hold on the past and the future is
precarious and my possession in my own time is always
postponed until a stage when I may fully understand it,
yet this stage can never be reached, since it would be
one more moment, bounded by the horizon, its future,
and requiring in its turn further developments in order
to be understood. My voluntary and natural life; therefore
knows that it merges into another power which stands
in the way of its completion, and gives it a permanently
tentative look' (Paul, 2006).

That other power is natural time, 'Natural time is always
there.' These poems exist in this provisional natural time
whether the poet is aged ten, nineteen or thirty two.
This in between world is always provisional and similar
to the construction of image and never more fluid than
from the moment it is realised. Working within it opens
up the possibility of both close observation and the

possibility of movement. *Intertextuality* continues as the world continues to turn. Unburdened by its own complexity it offers us a 'space' to capture provisionality through publication. The question nonetheless remains, how will these young poets view this book in ten, twenty or thirty years when the writers and image-makers have gone? Will the book have a life of its own in their own changing lives?

This 'in between world' is where creative tension lies, it includes and has its bearing in Being and in Time and exists in the world of transitions. Like every transition between the formal and informal it has a large territory of its own. It is often the place where we make sense of situations, no matter what our age in being exposed to different imaginary processes and identities. The recognition of this world has large implications not only for all the producers of text this book has involved but also illustrates the irrelevancies of age, physical space or indeed continent when it comes to making creative journeys. We would like to register our great thanks to Printmakers, Professional Writers and all our young poets represented here.

Susana Sambade
Tony Wailey
London College of Communication
University of the Arts.

Reading

Bordieu, P. (1998) 'Practical Reason', Stamford: Stamford University Press.

Deleuze, G. (2003 ed) 'Francis Bacon: Logic of Sensation', London: Continuum.

Eco, U. (2005 ed) 'The Poetics of the Open Work' in Hartley, J. Creative Industries, Oxford: Blackwell.

Earnshaw, S. (2007 ed) 'The handbook of creative writing', Edinburgh: University Press.

Harper, G. (2006) 'Teaching Creative Writing', London: Continuum.

Hunt, C. & Sampson, F. (2005 ed) 'The Self on the Page: Theory and Practice of Creative Writing in Personal Development', London: Jessica Kingsley.

Paul, K. (2006) Merleau-Ponty 'Phenomenology of perception', Routledge: Oxford.

Ricoeur, P. (2000) 'The Just', Illinois: University of Chicago Press.

Wenger, E. (2005) 'Communities of Practice', Cambridge: Cambridge University Press.

Wlodkowski, R. J. (1999) 'Enhancing adult motivation to learn: A comprehensive guide for teaching all adults', San Francisco: Jossey-Bass.

Contents

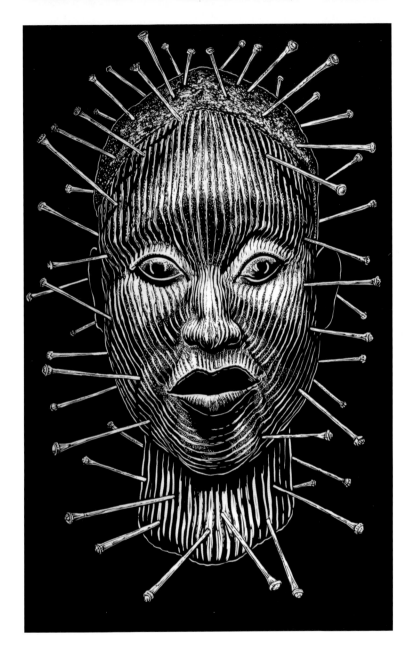

African Renaissance fetish
Jonathan Comerford

The face is my face,
Nails death has placed.
Pain is withheld as this provokes fear.
Fear that would turn into pointless tears.
Salty tears flowing fill my crevices of wounds
making them sting, more pain to my song.

Time passes and healing hands extract
leaving me to deal with scars forever etched
On my face, a reminder of deaths latest embrace.
When will he return or is he still lurking there hidden
where eyes cannot see? No, I won't let the fear
Nor the dread get the best out of me!
Better to love, laugh and dance,
Living each day as if it were the last.

Susana Sambade
Creative Writing Research
Associate Lecturer

The thorns of the white man's supremacy
pierce at my skin
Its hate penetrates my love
Its fear inflames my rage
Its deafness to my persecution and pain
I am pinned in the homelands of rejection
Bound with racism and prejudice
Apartness in body and race
Forced to live in segregation
Stripped of South African pride
Apartheid is my suffering
Black is my name.

Louise Happé
Exploring Creative Writing
BA Film and Video

A plain white canvas isolated in a cold dark room
Thick brush of colour swept across the page
Diluted clouds form in a liquid mixture
Frail hands trembling to achieve perfection
The eyes of the master, a mysterious world
The blinds split open, sunshine flickers
A smile awakens a sense of relief

What was once bland, tasteless, empty
Now filled with a thousand pins like the spikes
of a hedgehog.
Sharp in the dark, shiny like a pen
Stabbed across a lonely face
Hurt and sadness to be set free to escape
A world of pain and frustration
Into the new.

Kim Rose Lewis
Exploring Creative Writing
FDA Media Practice

Dark Visage etched in coal,
grimly beautiful emotionless stare.
Looking beyond or through the distance,
breaking the night with colours unseen
the persecuted but not helpless woman.
A look at ease hides the tenacity inside
Stabbing white scratches like lightning bolts
Strike features uncaring to the uncaring eye.
Thorns a barbwire halo for the face
a lasting impression, a far away race
the screaming gaze no longer screams but
Silently stares, draws you in.

Chris Harward
Exploring Creative Writing
FDA Media Practice

Nails in the head but never the soul
Mythologized and beatified at the expense of our own.

Live 8 didn't debate concrete slums and abject poverty
Or the forgotten jobless and hopeless of my society,
Only how to throw money at a problem,
This the answer to their naivety.

So they want to help the savage, Sir Bob and Co.
How ignorant they are of history, culture. They don't know.

Let people decide their own fate, fight for what they believe
Immobilise yourself in fraternity
Develop
Achieve Equality.

Does a continent forever need to be in debt,
To those whose forefathers had enslaved and kept?

I'll concentrate my anger on those whose minds,
Overdose, drown and swell,
With brands, labels, credit cards and cash.
Those that are told what to do

By those who look on the bottom of their shoe,
When they search for both me and you.

Michael Hughes
Exploring Creative Writing
BA Journalism

Mother and child reunion
Billy Mandindi

Their guns keep us apart, their hatred for one another,
their scorn, their sheer desire to abolish the other,
keep us apart. Men of metal bullet carriers guard
the lands that part us,
my child I miss you, miss you like the earth would
miss the sun moon and stars.
No matter what power I possess, your running away
has left my heart grey
Now you're alone in this land of war, should you be
dead, bulleted to death from tools
your father provides or has your identity led you to be
kidnapped and am I to await
a notice of ransom
Sleep is something I don't and won't attempt until you
are back with us my son
This holy war is full of winged angels with guns, taken
from me my land might be,
But spare my son, please just take me, why are you
crying mummy
That's how I felt when you were lost my prince, and
now all those that bought harm
around you will suffer our wrath
I promise to deliver you young prince the skulls of
everyman that wishes harm
against your head
Put your crown on now young prince and enter my
arms, your father wants to see you.

Leon Garwood
Exploring Creative Writing
BA Marketing & Advertising

Nine months of curiosity, excitement, happiness
And joy of what would be

Taken away causing pain, discomfort and a
Missing piece for the rest of ones life.

Those feelings of nine months thankfully given
Back when reunited with the new one,
Now the pain has gone you see

Megan Malekmian
BA Digital Media Production 3

Finally we are together again
Don't be upset
I've missed you mother
Don't be upset
We are away from the pain
Away from the hate

Mother, we can finally rest
Don't be upset
Mother no more stress
Don't be upset
We are now being looked after
By our fathers helpers

Mother, don't be afraid
Look up, they are here to stay
Don't be upset
Just hold me tight
Don't be upset
Let us sleep
Finally at peace we are alright.

Heba Keshk
Moving and Tuning History
BA Journalism

The fat old bloated, slimy snake slithered silently to its den.
The starved lizard lay poisoned to strike at its prey at half ten.
The pyramid stood, gasping as the first people in years ran inside.
The boy went that way because he didn't want to play that day.
The angels followed not wanting to thieve, also not wanting to grieve.
The birds sang out, cuddly and feathery, but come too close
And you will leave the mother, old but happy, sat thinking
Where her young son was, he rushes in, tired and breathless.
They had their meal, yummy without worry.

Oliver Jettoo
5N
Dog Kennel Hill School

The boy with the party hat,
Scared of his mother's eyes,
The owls in the wallflower trees,
Learning how to fly.
The guards of the pyramids,
Passing gracefully through the sky,
The birds the bees and the bumblebees
Don't bother me
I am a tree a bird and a bee.

Tommy Yapp
5N
Dog Kennel Hill School

Bomme Ba Rona (Our Mothers)
Madi Phali

My mum is the best!
My mum can be a pain
My mum can be nice
My mum can be no one less
Because she is mine
She can look like a mighty mess
And she can be a mighty pest
So now you know how lucky you are
If you have a mum like mine
Right!

Georgia-Blue Caddock
5E
Dog Kennel Hill School

My mother
She gets on my nerves,
But I love her.
She hits me
But I love her.
She's always there
when I need her.
I love her.
Been there my whole life
I love her.

Basirat Babajide
5E
Dog Kennel Hill School

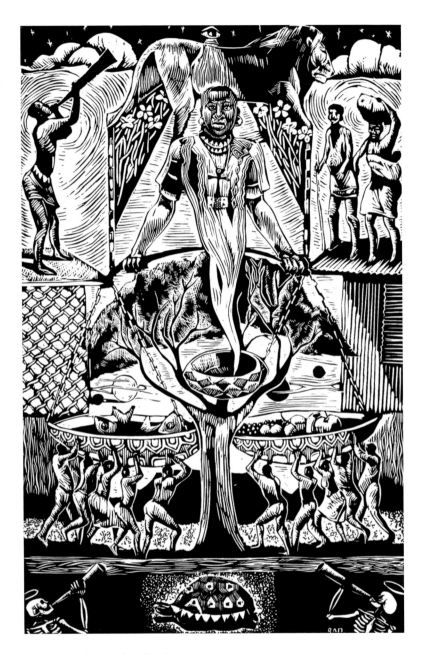

Rebirth, Arising, Awakening
Ricky Dyaloyi

Angels with battered wings
Hold their dangerous guns
The pyramid hides in shadow
Sharp, its mouth open
The Queen enters the dust
Full with disgusting webs
A mother looks for her son
She was ill but she was brave
The scary, slimy red snake
Slivering the slimy walls
The lizard's long tongue
Reaching from its lungs
The birds happy and loyal
Singing the royal song
The patterns still on the wall
Squared and flowered in patterns
The cross on her neck
Shining and blazy
She was ill, she was sweating
The holy crown of the dungeons
All rusty and dusty
The skeleton skull
That once was human
A statue still, she was ill
Scared in its dream
Bring us mercy sweet mother

Kelly Fitzgerald
5N
Dog Kennel Hill School

The magical spooky spirit controls every human's soul
Terrifying skeleton angels play music as they hurtle
To the concrete and sink beneath the earth.
The dead patterned turtle lay in his grave wriggling
Around, to the bottom of the ground.
Petrified bony men and women have boats to the spirits
In command,
A magical tree flowering and swaying in the breeze
Opens its arms, welcoming the morning rain
Trumpet players starved and exhausted blow out their last breaths
In the name of the spirits thick fog black and misty grips
The morning sunlight, screaming back off for the hurricane.

Amara Mighty
5N
Dog Kennel Hill School

Separated thoughts connect
World is splitting
In two halves
One half king
Rules one the other
Give up on me
Let me free
Yours is the ego black and white
Shivering yet bound tight
The cruelty of your right
Disguises me
Let me free
And both worlds be.

Anastasia Novikova
Exploring Creative Writing
FDA Photojournalism

The ring waking the god,
Owning it to the full.
Scales racing to see who,
Can weigh the most
It fruit or its Body
Skeletons blowing the flute,
Professional trying to wake the god.
The god is awakening and
Arising from his peaceful sleep,
The turtle slowly plodding up
to see the commotion,
Thinking it a herd of elephants.
The tree standing tall and proud,
Lifting the ring, holding the
Gods strongly, proudly, standing.
The flowers are growing and
Surrounding the god
With all their might
The eye is looking down,
At its child, their god,
Protecting the love with its glare.
Stars are lighting the sky,
Saying 'good morning God' sir.

Aidan Baker-Reynolds
5N
Dog Kennel Hill School

African Renaissance
Luthando Lupuwana

Genie, Genie, tell me more
About the future ever more.
Why should I
You have a tortoise 900 years old?
Genie, Genie, please.
I am blue and I can vanish
Into smoke no no, don't go.
Please stay I have cakes and grapes.
No, I shall not, you have devils
Angels with the same wings.
I am Master, I go when I please.
POOF POOF

Jack Turner
5N
Dog Kennel Hill School

Long Walk to Democracy
Solomon Siko

Freedom is…
Running, jumping freely
Expressing yourself
Enjoying life
Dancing around
Only doing what you see
Making all kinds of things

James Pagel
5E
Dog Kennel Hill School

Birds on a wire under the sun,
Fish in the sea having fun,
Boats sailing, people looking,
Catching the fish, I'll be cooking.

Jordan Whiting
5E
Dog Kennel Hill School

Praising Ancestors
Velile Soha

African music is like eating stew, yam,
Peppersoup, plantain, fofo, jolloh rice
African music is like listening to difference
Kind of African
African music is like dancing to the rhythm
of drums, happily playing in the sunshine
African music is like eating fried rice
African music is like watching OBE and BENTV
African music is spontaneous
African music is my life
African music is when the sun shines upon the
African people and tribes
African music is in my blood

Adetola Adeyanju
5E
Dog Kennel Hill School

A still rounded pot sits like a frog,
On a blazing fire with roaring arms outstretched and
wrapping round the pot.
The two wise old men stand frozen,
Their eyes flickering.
The sharp, bent fence leans towards the men,
And the stones around the fire, that look like rolling
hills,
Begin to go a boiling red, then an unbearable white.
The ancient cloaks they wear,
Flap like wings in the breezing air.
The patterns on the pot dance before their eyes,
The small straw hats in the distance are forever
yawning for they have no doors.
The men hold smooth wooden poles,
Which they use to stir the formula in the pot.
They smell dry hot land,
They see the crackling sun,
They feel scorching grass beneath their feet.
They are praising ancestors.

Lila Bernstein-Newman
5N
Dog Kennel Hill School

Rhythm of Revival
Vuyile Vuyiye

Here she comes with steady beat
The pounding keys repeat their chores
Can you hear the mumbled drums
The echo's fifth of every chord
Lose yourself in dripping bass
A stripped down pulse
In fractured air
Bleed dry the skies
And raise those arms
Offload into every soul
Absorb that song and dance a spill
That fills the swelling chests to brim
Beads of nature's sweat descend
A smile that will not wash away

Jamie Veltman
Moving and Tuning History
BA G.M.D. Typography

A pregnant women is boiling and resting
In the burning sun, her thoughts but one.
A hand frozen and reaching for its prey.
As if to say I am a man happy and excited,
Beckoning his children all as one.
But a shadow filled with doom and fright
Painting out a wail of silence.
A shadow that would love to sail.
But they are all here in the same atmosphere
And they are all thinking of a path.
Entirely of dread with deep black shadows
Dancing around them, it waves to them
All one more time and waits
For them to expect it.

Saskia Collyns
5N
Dog Kennel Hill School

Precious life
Zan Louw

When our fathers held us
in our arms, they were
separated by their colour
but we saw no colour
at least not for a while
then later as we grew
we knew what we knew
our minds nudged
and pulled, tweaked
and our eyes grew
to see only differences
between us.
That you liked lazy days
and dusty stoops
worrying the beetles
I could not see
that you liked winging
through the fields
with your arms hooped
I could not see
at ten when you stood at
the top of our road
down towards our house
looking at me.
Everything was mine
Still I could not see
everything was easy
what a different world
you lived in as we
grew into women.
Now I see you clearly
my child smiles at yours
I wish I'd known you
then.

Emma Flynn
Exploring Creative Writing
BA G.M.D. Illustration

Children, children dark and white
Children, children nice and bad
Children, children bold and scared
Children, children loved and cared
Children, children play and shout
Children, children tall and short
Children, children happy forever

Connor Manners
5E
Dog Kennel Hill School

Birds singing peacefully
River is a piece of silk
The sunshine fills the sky
The man holds a baby girl
A little face pops up
Herons eat fishes.
This is a new world for me.
Hello everyone.

Phoebe Neal
5N
Dog Kennel Hill School

Eenheid (togetherness)
Sophie Peters

Women watching
Grandmas staring
Children gasping
Sun amazed
Houses frightening
Animals shocked
Clothes alarmed
Plants startled
Clouds nervous
What is it?

Temi Lawal
5E
Dog Kennel Hill School

Angel, are you an angel?
Noiselessly you come down to earth,
Give us your good luck, beautiful angel.
Everything you do for us beautiful angel.
Lovely, kind, beautiful, angel.

Phoebe Finn
5E
Dog Kennel Hill School

Communal print

Communal

The world is a big busy place
My mother always said to me,
She said 'You've got to be careful,
The world is a busy place'.
My mother always said to me,
She said 'People are swinging and dinging,
The world is a busy place'.
My mother always said to me,
She said 'People hold fish with you,
I just don't want to know'.
The world is a busy place.
My mother always said to me…
Now I believe her.

Anon
5N
Dog Kennel Hill School

So many countries
So many differences
Nothing alike
How about a bite
Like when to fly a kite
In the windy weather

Anon
5N
Dog Kennel Hill School

I am relaxation with action.
I am the tree silhouetted by sunlight.
I am different but I am the same
I am boats tho' I am water
I am the fish who have no fins
I am cold and boiling rivers.
I am a bird with no feathers
I am Africa.

Iris Mathieson
5N
Dog Kennel Hill School

New Home: Cutting grass
Robert Siwangaza

Here is a mum waking up at 4am
Going to the field
To fetch straw but forgot about the hen
They live in a hut that has no bed
the children don't even get to play with ted
Their mother is poor, tired and weak
Here is a mum not looking like a wreck

Sam Djehi-Bi
5E
Dog Kennel Hill School

Cracked waves flow across her face
Ghosts of smiles fade her eyes
Madame Sun kissed too hard too long

Her drift wood lips sit deep and firm
Other's secrets locked away for good
Words become stronger with time spent alone

A cliff edge chest keeps her solid
With shredded hands she works the grain
On leather feet she grows dusty in another day

Time has been tough

Hugo Donkin
Exploring Creative Writing
FDA Media Practice

The long stringy grass flowing through the breeze
I am a tall pointy mountain, a windy day searching for
my prey.
I am the swinging sliding door of the longhaired
houses.
I am a woman busy and hard working looking after
crops.
I am the windows of a house with eyes that glare.

Julia Francis-Owusuasefa
5N
Dog Kennel Hill School

New Home: Thatching roof
Robert Siwangaza

Backwards and forwards collecting grass
Up a ladder down a ladder up and down side to side
Collecting and cutting
It takes two not one to thatch a roof
Cutting grass all day must be hard
To Work all day
Thirst and hunger
Sun is beaming
Birds are singing
At last the sun is down and now is sleeping
Been together all day long
Harmony, peace and now is happy, now is silence

Danielle Harris
5E
Dog Kennel Hill School

I am building a new home
My old one was in ancient Rome
But I want to go home
To get my Afro comb because
Over here it isn't fair
I have to carry water on my head
I don't even have a bed
We build our house out of straw
And nothing more
Our roof isn't even water proof
It is nothing more than only straw
I am very lonely and this
Has just crushed my dreams
No ponies here
Crushed my dreams it seems.

Isaac Robinson
5N
Dog Kennel Hill School

New Home: How proud
Robert Siwangaza

This is for you
Our home is our castle
Your day is long
I took this vow
My word is my bond
Nurture this love
Feed from my breast
My spirit is strong
I trust in you
To sow your seeds
Bathed in the rain
Fed by our sun
In here to serve you
I am your Queen
Your desire
Your passion
Your pain

Amanda Miles
Exploring Creative Writing
FDA Journalism

Indada isuka ifele (Father cleaning skins)
Robert Siwangaza

I've watched these trees grow from naïve seeds,
Into weeping willows that cry in the breeze,
But the sounds that occur from these beautiful drums,
Are of happiness and strength, and of peace and love,
There's no effort in my smile when I'm free like this,
I see planes overhead heading for the abyss,
The sky is my ceiling and this ground is my stage,
yet this life that I live shows me signs of a cage,
The unity that joins us is far and between,
The sound that it carries me keeps my state of mind clean,
But the time that it takes for us all to sing together,
Is long so I'll keep this mind state forever.

Shane Connolly
Moving and Tuning History
BA Sound Arts and Design

I've given you my time and efforts
I've given you my life and presence
But do I regret it… No
Now it's finally my time and no effort
My life in my own presence.
This day seemed far away
But now that it's here
What do I do throughout the day?
I'll just sit here and watch the world flash by
Let it get busy with time and effort
I'll just sit here and make time my pleasure

Jaime Sanchez
Moving and Tuning History
BA Marketing and Advertising

Drinking ritual
Robert Siwangaza

Taste the ritual
Wet the lips
With ceremony

Decorum flows
Pending decision
Formality waits
Counting minutes

For every drop
With bated breath
Awaits approval

Omo Umoru
Creative Writing
BA Book Arts

Happy Birthday to you
Happy Birthday to my mum
Happy Birthday to you
My mum is 98 again
She was 98 last year
No one knows how she does it
But I know
She drinks a special water
It's called a Dinage drink for oldies
Happy Birthday to you
Happy Birthday to mum
You look 21 but you're really 92

Evan Shonfield
5E
Dog Kennel Hill School

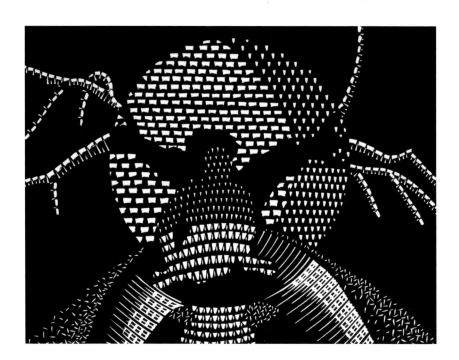

Come morning I
Vuyilile Vuyiye

Awake: unclasp lead hooks from eyelids swaying,
And pour parched hope from an aching throat,
Sink sore fingertips, amidst cool shadows,
Of lank rushes, and nodding reeds.
Bask in the pools warm copper midst,
And coax the plains dry slumbering hum.
Break daylight from earths well thumbed shell,
Banish conspiring pleats of black, back beyond,
Come Morning I. At last.

Harry Darby
Exploring Creative Writing
BA Film and Video

Sun rose this morning
Just to greet me
The moon lingered
Happy to see me
The land is free
I am with she
It's a new dawn
I am living

Nina Welch
Exploring Creative Writing
BA Sound Arts and Design

At the start of the tunnel,
Fingers clenched into a fist,
The anticipation and excitement
You can't seem to resist!

With your heart beating faster,
You don't think of time,
When exhilarated and satisfied,
You'll step off the ride.

It's about long drives,
With droplets of water,
Thrown from the sea,
Broken on my windshield.

Walking in the cold,
A disillusioning road,
The starlight cafes,
Water, curdling at my toes.

It's smoky rooms,
And hazy memories,
Shadows cast
By lingering trees.

As the story unfolds,
It's like the beginning of time.
Pointless conversations
Late into the night.

With your heart beating faster,
You're unaware of time,
Unexpecting and unsatisfied,
You'll be thrown off the ride!

And like any end
We just have to succumb,
by holding on tight,
Until morning comes…

Chandni Mehta
Creative Writing
FDA Design For Graphic Communication

Not Unworthy of…
S Williamson

Look at things from my point of view
From my side, where I see you
With your pale white face
And your light eyes, blind.
Unseeing, blinded and narrow minded.

Move and take another standpoint
Stand over there and look again
Gaze into my dark eyes,
Imagine the feel of my pure, black skin
Prejudice - keep away.

Mary Pullen
Exploring Creative Writing
BA Book Arts

Rolling the barrel
Kweti Nzubi

Man rolling barrel up a twisting road
The houses wave goodbye
A gate waits for its supper
Like a lion on the prowl.
Villagers huddle around the fire
It dances in the moonlight
The barrel tries to run away
The green bush grass
Tries to reach the man.
The man walks on.

Farah Mohammed
5N
Dog Kennel Hill School

Vukani (Early risers)
Ricky Dyaloyi

Tightly packed voices lift through the golden sands of time,
Hailing to those who have yet shed the two-sided tear of tribulation.
Take this tiny voice of mine and let it be heard across land and ocean
Telling of a story that may never yet come to be.
The words tumble and lift resonating through the passages of many ears –
Will they be heard over the hum of adversity and fear?
Such strength there is in a single voice but the chorus of many
Withstands the test of adversity.

Alison Ross
Moving and Tuning History
BA Marketing and Advertising

Midnight antics
Jonathan Comerford

Steel Planes, Killer flames.
Now War Unseen. We ain't fools.
New age? A new Rage.

Gareth Carolan
BA Digital Media Production 3

What a full moon night?!
The battle between you and me…
Who is going to survive?
Who'll win the fight
Who is going to die?
Die without breath on a rocky road…

Cho Lee
BA Digital Media Production 3

Planes can be cruel
And planes can be cool
Planes can fall
But for girls they're a mall.
Planes in light
Planes in the night
Planes that fight
But I can't imagine
Planes that bite.

Barney Aldridge
5N
Dog Kennel Hill School

Uncle Sam diverting planes
Eclipse covers the blinding blaze
Hanging on for dear life

Stephen Perkins
BA Digital Media Production 3

The sound of the aeroplane makes me feels alive
And happy and free
And the sun makes me feel nice and relaxed
Why are people arguing over the sky?

Makeda Notice
5E
Dog Kennel Hill School

Too tall men
Strong and brave
Stopping a plane
And feel no pain

Floating in the sky
Stars blazing bright
Two tall men
Pulling with all their might
I wonder what they're trying to achieve

Xanthe Greenwood
5E
Dog Kennel Hill School

Bloody shame
Cry! African women
Smouldering red glow from within
Bowels of dark African chiefdoms
Snail pace development
Creeping red ribbons
Lions in bows are collecting
Skulls and bones meat rotten
Hyenas laugh
Gnawing remains
Crushed ribs
Destroyed lives
Aids and blood

Jaco Marias
Exploring Creative Writing
BA Journalism

Storm seas covering the dark
Water splashing over the lion.
Light fishing in bright water
For the moment to kill a sailor.
Light fishing in their eyes
Falling down into the sea.

Ediz Tasher
5N
Dog Kennel Hill School

Detention
Billy Mandindi

Look at me in shackles and chains you can take away
my freedom but not the
One in my brain

You've got typical views of me because I've been
arrested but whether its
Crimes of passion or sin is neglected.

My eyes are not mirrors so my pain's not reflected.

I'm overcome with oppression forced into a mind state
where most wish to
Keep me until my soul breaks.

You may have me in custody but we are yet to
determine my fate I stand strong
Whilst surrounded by hate.

There's no need to ask we all have regrets it's what we
choose and what we are
Willing to accept.

It's all standard and casual for these policemen I bet.

Lock me up throw away the key send me to darkness
where you can't hear my
Plea.

Am I innocent or not? I really can't say but just like
taxes I've got no choice
But to pay.

Could I change things on that unfaithful day? I ask
this to my father every time
I pray.

Letitah Obiri
Exploring Creative Writing
BA Journalism

Who is being killed?
What exactly is being said?
A vision of only Black and white
An empty canvas bruised and torn
Standing in the waiting line
Hearing nothing but my sorry past

I stand alone in my own company
A toy soldier waiting to be knocked down
An illness waiting, the worst yet to come

Standing
There seems to be no one else
Surrounded
Yet on my own
a motionless wheel moving no where
The Truncheon
Security, safety or a weapon
The daily act of authority

Victoria Berry
Exploring Creative Writing
BA Marketing & Advertising

The police came looking for me
With their truncheons and guns
Saying I stole pie, what a lie
They said they put me behind bars
Lucky I had a knife and fork tho'
I could cut a hole in the pole but
the knife and fork just shattered
I want to get out but I don't know
I just don't know how

Anon
5N
Dog Kennel Hill School

A slave,
A prisoner,
A faceless product of the system
Like the sheep they've turned me into,
I simply follow the crowd.
An obligation to follow the orders
the racist superiors,
I have no mind of my own.

I live my life as governed
made aware of how the colour
the skin affects my quality, my life
I too am shackled
I am the guy whose colleagues
enjoy demeaning the black man.

Cheneen Williams
Exploring Creative Writing
FDA Journalism

Sgt Bob's rent boys were glad to carry me away,
Even after explaining I was caught in the affray.
They gave me a name ending in seven,
The judge has said I will be getting eleven.
And what for exactly I hear you cry?
It was not me but that did not satisfy.
Instead they dress me in wrong pinstripes today,
You must have been confused by Savile Row's display.
So what is the problem officer? You want me to
perform?
Surely this is unjust; for a bigot in a uniform.

Marcus Muir
Moving and Tuning History
FDA Interior Design

I cried
I remember I fell on my knees and
I cried

With one hand
I wiped my tears
The other hand held my fathers voice

He said
'He seemed fine,
 Strong,
 So don't you cry
 He wont be there for long'

Did you cry?
When you saw the flashing lights
And when they read you your rights

Did you cry?
Look into his eyes
What did you see?

Do you see a criminal?
Do you see a troubled soul?
Do you see the chances slip by?
I gave you my hand
But you brushed it away

I gave you my heart
But you pushed it aside
The strangest thing whatever you do
You'll always have my hand
To raise you high

Sarah Mwangi
Moving and Tuning History
BA Journalism

Misfortune defied your achievements
Bringing the rules of the law,
As your acts become inexcusable
For those who reign the world.

You may think you haven't done anything,
You may say that you weren't wrong.

To the spot where the events had happened
Uniformed officials have to come
To take you to the place
Where the freedom has a grievance.

Guillermo Clemente
Exploring Creative Writing
FDA Media Practice

One man is getting arrested
Black and white
Ghana
The men are wearing uniform

Mr Police Officer
Is where are you take me
Mr Police Officer
What did I do?

Mr Police Officer
Why are you take me
Mr Police Officer

David Maxwell
5E
Dog Kennel Hill School

Yo Yo Yo give me your money.
What's that sound?
Sorry I'm on the run.
They're coming.
AAAAAA! I fainted.
The next thing I know
I am in detention.
Here is my song.
Yo Yo give me your money.
I am going home to my honey.
Is that my friend Jill
Coming over the hill?
There is my best friend.
Will this world ever end?

Reece Edwards
5E
Dog Kennel Hill School

They got me.
They chased me.
I only stole a PSP and TV.
I'm scared! I'm scared!

Taigh McCarthy-Faussett
5E
Dog Kennel Hill School

Oh no, the police got me
red handed. Oh no, this is going to go
In my record book.
Oh no, I am a bad boy.
Oh no, my mum is going to hear about this.
Oh no, I have a cell with no man in it.
I am in DETENTION

Josiah Parchment-James
5E
Dog Kennel Hill School

I see the policemen
I see one man
Is I Billy Somebody
The man is angry
But what is he thinking
Is I why me
Why said it be
That insult policeman
He is angry as I am
A man writing script
Like a zebra got 5 numbers
All of them are 16357
I am an ugly man
And you don't want to
Mess with me

Dominator
5N
Dog Kennel Hill School

Life in these shackles
Just because my skin
Is darker than yours
My world! My world! is
Black and white stripes

Thick chains cutting though my flesh
A daily taste of my master's batten
Beating and pounding my body
OUT! OUT! I must get out
It is too dark a sentence

My meal, which I get once a day
I swear it might be my last
The last I'll ever have
A meal that strangles me

A desperate call for aid and yet
It strangles me
I have been here far too long
OUT! OUT! I will get OUT
I can taste freedom

Fabian Cloete
Foundation Programme Graphic Design
Cape Peninsula University of Technology
Cape Town, South Africa

Gold canvas tempus for hustler gentiles,
Caught in the monopoly play of Marxists
Political law and oppressive progression
Trying to enforce slave regression
All it brings is mass detention

Wooden batons play upon broken souls
Naked bodies thrown in vans
And made to dance.
Electrical strings play neon lights,
Metal scenery with a mechanical touch
Birthed on tainted soil, metal stone huts
Broken doors and there is much more.

Blue hats strategically pursuing blacks
A system instilling fear, keeping the check
Police dogs attacks and maul
Pimps galore selling out the cloth
From which they were sewn.
Blacks danced all the way to detention
Why we beat them more.

Tabiso Njamela
Foundation Programme Graphic Design
Cape Peninsula University of Technology
Cape Town, South Africa

Knights
Billy Mandindi

The dark glare of the sky, with symbols of the sun,
Spears like the moon and holding a shield
South Africa plays.
Standing, guarding the planets and stars
Pressing them like trousers
Black and white for Christians they would see
With help from the knight he'll let them free.
Stripes on the shield like cat whiskers.
Save other people.
The knight
The knights
The knights that light the moon.

Benjamin Moston
5E
Dog Kennel Hill School

'Yo, Yo man whaas up,' yelled the knights
A hippy with a head like brick wall struts by.
The armed knights stare in amazement
The seaside plants explode.
The two knights attack their own queen
As the happy expired man walks by.
'Was happin dooood?' one of the knights asks
A depressed cat looks at them tiredly.
The knights stare at the old wall as
A hungry rude boy has a good long glare.

Tom O'Brien
5N
Dog Kennel Hill School

Prayer
Billy Mandindi

My God is a big black spirit and hip life,
My God speaks in tongue of Twi,
My God, Ghanaian God, in the world of church music,
My God speak in soulful sound of the church choir.
My God is like a mountain of sweets.
My God is a special person of light to my heart.
My God is a wonderful God to me.

Dona Korang-Awua
5E
Dog Kennel Hill School

I serve the light
It keeps me from harm
My hands raised in faithful prayer
Searching for your guidance.

Gaenor Barends
Foundation Programme Graphic Design
Cape Peninsula University of Technology
Cape Town, South Africa

It is the gift God gave for us to use
To pray for those who need it most
It is the most powerful weapon against all evil
And the best way to overcome fear
I pray, do you?

Gary Abrahams
Foundation Programme Graphic Design
Cape Peninsula University of Technology
Cape Town, South Africa

On my knees I pray, these words I say,
To U Lord give me strength to face this day.
For this is a cold world in which I stay
But to you Lord by your side I must pray
With you and I trust, blow my dark days away
Bless us with your touch, take this heart of rust
Purify it and make it white as snow
The cross of life I'll carry
It is heavy, I will fall
But with these palms together
My knees to the ground
I will rise
By you I was found.

Ryan Africa
Foundation Programme Graphic Design
Cape Peninsula University of Technology
Cape Town, South Africa

Wood breathes through the lines carved deep,
Held up by silver spears of light.
Oaks strong skin, a still soul breathes.
Times trail, wakes carved sight.

Senses peel to the core
Roots of seeds sown, blind light
Oak's strong skin, a still soul breathes
Distant echoes strike a winding flight

The mind left the body's shore
Tight skins beat the plight
Oak's strong skin, a still soul breathes
Timeless tale holds rhythms of night

Melody Renouf
Exploring Creative Writing
BA Photography

Dear Father; I drown in tears and pools of blood
I want your people to shine so I call to you
Misplaced energy and overactive molecules flood
Blood veins of the native
Color displacement was the spell removed
Apartheid still lives like a chronic wound it's the real
Pandemic
In minority the majority of urban communities are
Segregated
Decided and altered destinies, us the youth suffer
Consistently
From unprescribed drugs we die
From unauthorized club and pub entry we die
But most of all we die from this
'survival of the fittest' mentality.
So I pray for a dream tonight and every night
To escape these nightmares, I'm tired and have no
More strength to fight
Imprisoned by society, the anxiety of tall walls that
Incarcerate us
I just want a ticket to sit in the front row seats
In Heaven, away from this parasite of a community,
Yes! death is the unity
most of our population lives in prison
Gone missing, shut out from the world
The rate of involuntary blood donation increases
The rate of tears dropping to the ground increases,
The rate of breath taken before time increases
And the rate of mother and children's swollen cheeks
Increases
Praying not to complain, but plead that we no longer
Bleed but grow in seeds and satisfied needs
So sad a song but someone must sing it
So testing a life but someone must live it.

AMEN

Viwe Mfaku
Foundation Programme Graphic Design
Cape Peninsula University of Technology
Cape Town, South Africa

Dear God my father
It's me again my Lord
Your child amongst many of your children
Come and save us my lord
Living in this world is hard
Jealousy and hatred abound
Come and show us the way Father
Without you we have no future
O' Lord above all things
Please hear me now
In life, in death and in suffering
I want to feel your presence
Deep down inside my soul
Please hear me now, O' Lord
AMEN.

Asanda Qumelwana
Foundation Programme Graphic Design
Cape Peninsula University of Technology
Cape Town, South Africa

Taking care
Billy Mandindi

Why neglect instead of uniting: who knows?
See how some of this might happen to you.
Or maybe someone close, you'd be terrified
How would you take care?

The easiest thing. Why make it difficult?
Why, it's so simple and natural
I strongly believe that you can make a difference
By turning night into day

Blue skies turn to cloud for those whose every day
Is the same, for those who cannot see past shadows?
To the sun on the other side
For those who have lost faith or are cold inside
Pray they don't stay lonely

Simo Langeni
Foundation Programme Graphic Design
Cape Peninsula University of Technology
Cape Town, South Africa

Hear, speak, see no evil
Billy Mandindi

We are unable to hear, speak and see.
We are the same in different ways.
The ways which we are not allowed to be
In the senses which have no opinions.
Difference,
We are different triplets.
Different opinions, the same colour.
The colour of patterns and currents.
The patterns swim their own sea.
But we are family.

Kunyarat Prom-Apiban
Exploring Creative Writing
BA Marketing & Advertising

Our life is good
We all hear it
Freedom of speech continues
United we speak without fear
Our rights are upheld
Together we see it
But wait…
Why can he not hear
Or she not speak
Or me not see
Is our life so good
our rights upheld
are we all so free.

Simon Jackson
Exploring Creative Writing
FDA Sports Journalism

Time was – we could see
We could see many different lives and colours
We could see pain
We could see light and hope
Then came rain.

Time was – we could hear
We could hear drums and bells singing
We could hear sighing
We could hear laughter and joy
Then came dying.

Time was – we had senses
We could feel warmth and flesh and passion
We could feel fear
We could feel comfort and pleasure
Then came tears.

Time was – we had tongues
We could speak freely and tell stories
We could tell lies
We could paint our histories and identities
Then came cries.

Time was – we were one
We could put on the masks of Janus
We could be good
We could reflect a giving and generous spirit
But…
Then came evil.

Marilyn McMenemy
Acting Head of College (2007–2008) LCC
University of the Arts London

I remember the proud wound that he wore to say I
played the game as well.
Yet I couldn't see or remember the sweetness of his
murder
But only all his sweetness piled into a death stare and
a smile that carried
all his mood without fail.
The myth of the hero he did not represent as he lay
there dying and
others ran on top of him further.

Blood is spattered daily on his face yet today directly
from his sweet heart.
He may have uttered a few words and it seemed that
he was proud to carry
his morals to this fall.
He bled to his early death and held within him all the
nation's fears
pushing through him like a sharp dart.
I saw as the sun slowly left his cheek and then aimed
herself at another
Political doll.

All this had been for everyone else to see, speak, and
see yet who was hearing,
the aching burns to his skin?
I was standing there and so were you.
Who was watching him gurgle his blood in his mouth?
I was standing there and so were you.
Who was shouting loud enough to end his misery and
bring his youthfulness and not let him sink?
I was there and so were you.

Nadia Al-Dhahir
Exploring Creative Writing
BA Media & Cultural Studies

Three people standing there
With their mouths shut
And one covering his eyes.
They're looking at you with
Their big bold yellow and
Green eyes like some mouldy
Egg and cheese.

Jinon Bartlett
5N
Dog Kennel Hill School

I am the shell you hold up to your ear,
I am the waves that you sometimes hear,
I am bells in the bell towers ringing,
I am a choir which is always singing,
Cup your ear and sense something near,
I am the one and only hearer.

I am the silence you hear at meals,
I am the calls that frighten the seals,
I am the one, who helps you shout,
I am the one, who blurts things out,
You cup your mouth you sound very bleak,
I am the one and only speak.

I am the one, who helps you see darkness,
I am the one, who sees people's laughter,
I am the one who sees no evil
I am the one who sees the flight
I am the one and only sight.

Anon
5N
Dog Kennel Hill School

Losing one's head
Billy Mandindi

Stark black and white prints, all with individual dramas
of their own happening inside
This particular one, though, is like a blow to the head
The character's and mine. Everything about it is
powerful to the eye, the patterns on the clothing he
wears, vibrant formations of the dots and lines, and
the energy shown in the handless arms snapped
apart, a chain shattered as a result. The image is
solid and thick, yet the fabric pattern provides some
relief from the block of black. It is unclear as to
the exact message Mandindi is trying to convey yet
perhaps it is one of political restraint versus freedom.
There is something of forceful power lying in it. The
crown on the loose head slightly echoes of the Alice
in Wonderland and the Queen's orders for one to lose
their head.
Those words scared me as a child and though it is
wonderfully crafted, this image will haunt me a little
now, too.

Charlotte Evans
Creative Writing
BA G.M.D. Illustration

The peaceful god she sleeps in chains,
The peaceful god she feels my pain.
The peaceful god she wants to dance,
The peaceful god she's in a trance.
The peaceful god she holds her head,
The peaceful god she might turn dead.
Peaceful god I'll break your chains,
Peaceful god I'll stop your pain.

Greta Sharp
5E
Dog Kennel Hill School

Losing one's head to find peace but all I got instead is this piece
Of heavy chain and bound to struggle to lose one's head
To find peace is never enough to wear it on your shirt; to make a statement can sometimes miss the point
to feel the Pain of Oppression is to leave ones self behind.
Freedom for your next of kin to carry on the peaceful load
So one does not lose one's head carrying these pieces of heavy heads
that weigh on head-time for peace to rest, loads will have to get lighter
To find new lighter fuel then real peace.

Theo Calliste
Moving and Tuning History
FDA Interior Design

I am headless, I am headless.
I am a headless horseman.
I will get my axe and chop
Chop your head off.
See if you can get mine.

Theo Thompson
5N
Dog Kennel Hill School

God save the African queen
Billy Mandindi

She is proud, a sight of sheer beauty and splendour.
She is the African Queen.
Rich golden fields outline her curves, her hair the
humid forest of Ghana.
Her voice is carried on the hot billowing winds; tribal
songs of yesterday.
She moves swiftly to the beat of the boar-skin drums
at her processions,
entrancing all who know her.
Her king is the proud lion, fearsome yet brave, he
pays the utmost respect.
She bears the raw scars of a painful past, yet she
smiles and forgives.
Her background is steeped in culture and tradition.
Her subjects have nothing but possess the addition.
She does not live in a large palace, nor does she ride
in a gold carriage.
They have stripped her riches but not her crown jewel
of pride.
She is Africa.

Letitiah Obiri
Exploring Creative Writing
FDA Journalism

Me and my posse is well hard
Me can write poems that will give you a dirty look
Me and my posse don't listen to R'n'B or grim
Me and my posse drink wine
Me and my posse are an ancient tribe
Me and my posse don't like to cry.
Me and my posse.

Adetola Adeyanja
5E
Dog Kennel Hill School

Together we stand united
Fearless, strong and brave
To protect our one so precious
Indeed we fight to save

For she has suffered long enough
To keep our mere existence
Her grace, beauty and pureness
Lies in her proud resistance

She must stay in her rightful place
No castle made by man
For she has blessed this very soil
Upon this sacred land

Serina Durant
Exploring Creative Writing
BA Media and Cultural Studies

God save the African Queen,
To give her money to the poor.
To look after children when they are ill,
To lead the Zulu warriors in battles.
To be the head teacher
To be strong in hard situations.
To be kind to other people when sad.
Now she is in prison.
What kind of Queen is she?
The African Queen.
May God bless the African Queen.

Dana Korup
5E
Dog Kennel Hill School

Save her to guide us
Save her from all her pains
Mkhusele kuzo zonke izinto
Bring her the light, show her the way
Bring all the memories of
Our Green Land… AFRICA…
As the look in her eyes that
Cries in fear of failure
Msondeze kubantu bakhe
Reunite her with her roots
She has served so many mixed minds
Let her rule our green AFRICA
As mother of the Land
Ebambe imibala yase AFRICA
entliziyweni yakhe
Serving her sentence
Give us the colour of AFRICA
God save the African Queen

Gunashe Koyana
Foundation Programme Graphic Design
Cape Peninsula University of Technology
Cape Town, South Africa

I dream
To see my Nubian queen
Freed
From mans wicked need
God grant her back her power
Before Satan's dogs devour

I remember the sound of love
And now all I hear is hate

The same people she breathed love into
Now suffocate

And we walk blindly the wilderness.

The pray
I dream
To see my Nubian queen
Freed
From mans wicked need
God grant her back her power
Before Satan's dogs devour

She once walked the same children hand in hand
Now they walk with hands in bondage

Every time she's disrespected
Neglected
A chain is tied around her body

When will she break free
When will she break free

The pray
I dream
To see my Nubian queen
Freed
From mans wicked need
God grant her back her power
Before Satan's dogs devour

African queens, we are their mothers
Sisters why do they hurt us so

Our circle demeana
Has us chasing yesterdays plight

The key, the answer lies in every woman
To break free from mans oppression
And realize our rights

The pray
God save our African queen.

Alessandro Kellier
Creative Writing
FDA Marketing and Advertising

We praise them, why do we need to?
They believe that they will be protected
From their enemies they do not face their fears.
We call them queens. Why?
Why do they need to have guards to protect them?

Other people lose their life to protect them
Why do the guards have to carry the knifes, spears,
Knopkjiers and all those heavy weapons?
If queens don't face up to challenges and their fears
What if we left them a day or month to face their
tears?

Let them be in those hands and crafts for days
Why do they have to make other people suffer for
their lives?
They have crowns on their heads for us to bow to
them.
Let us not protect them, because no-one can protect
them from death
We are not God, just human beings - here for a couple
of years

We too will die
We can only ask God to save the African Queen for us
Africa is a place for queens with dignity and respect
Africa is our country full of cultures and only queens
who look natural
God save the African Queens for our country not its
vultures

Vutivi Maluleke
Foundation Programme Graphic Design
Cape Peninsula University of Technology
Cape Town, South Africa

I am the African Queen with all my guards
The war has begun.
They are waiting to have peace and freedom
When they have the battle won
They will go to the church to pray for freedom.

Tolu Thomas
5E
Dog Kennel Hill School

Beautiful and natural Queen everyone admires
Beautiful Queen that everyone will share
Even if God asked for her

Please God save this Queen full of difficulty
Wars, strikes, pains, hates and cries
Help her inner conflict

God save the African Queen
From confrontation and bring light to her
A light which can turn to jubilation

That being born by this Queen
To live a happy life without any harm
That Light I call freedom

The Freedom that can be used to create
A new 'rainbow nation'
For the new generation

Simthandile Jantjies
Foundation Programme Graphic Design
Cape Peninsula University of Technology
Cape Town, South Africa

May God save you
Every step that you take
May he guide you
Each decision you make
May he help you
When life gets rough
May he lift you
When you fall

God save the African Queen
When life gets colder
May God save you
As you grow older
May God be with
The African Queen

Xolani Hlwele
Foundation Programme Graphic Design
Cape Peninsula University of Technology
Cape Town, South Africa

WARNING
Billy Mandindi

Two guardians, of different kith and kin,
Yet of the same face – what cruel fortune is this?
You elude me with your foreshadowing –
A serpent entwined with a lute,
Snails meeting, fish on wood.
A man would need the vision of Teiresias
To hold this semblance of truth.
And what of the skull and bones that haunts the centre?
such an obvious omen to obvious conclusions?
I pray against it.
The oracle is in their eyes –
The priest, the Christian, the shaman, the African.
a high wall of black that hides their hearts.
Now I see the fish line the coffin. A sea death?
God knows and reminds me I know nothing.
Away you friendly snails, I will know thy meaning yet.

Komal Verma
Exploring Creative Writing
BA Film and Video

I dare you to play the guitar
With the snake wrapped round it.

I dare you to smack the bones
And make it cry.

I dare you to eat the snails
And make it small.

I dare you to pop the man's brains out
And make them real.

Rommel Chambers
5E
Dog Kennel Hill School

Bang, Bang, Bang.
Shame who died was it you or was it me?
Or was it someone who was angry who
Was buried in the sand?
Maybe it was a man who played with snakes.
Maybe he was a man who eats slugs and snails.
Maybe he is still alive.
Maybe he is really dead.
maybe the skeleton is his death.

Peter Matthew Thompson
5E
Dog Kennel Hill School

The music I can hear is coming from that guitar
But what's inside that makes it so enchanting?
It's a skull and a snake wrapped round the top,
I am being hypnotised by the eyes of musicians,
I fall into a deep sleep then I wake up
And I am in the safety of my own home
Lying in my bed,
But then I hear the music again and again.
Was I dreaming or was it REAL?

Cecily Cook
5E
Dog Kennel Hill School

WARNING don't touch me, I am highly explosive
But I live, WARNING don't look at me, I'll melt you
With my fiery eyes. WARNING don't smell me.
I smell like toxic gas strong enough to kill an elephant
I sit on my bone throne awaiting my meat
My guards are strong and run without stopping
To eat you WARNING. My eye is a small pupil
But as strong and tall like a tower. Do you know me?
I'm the evil snail.

Nathan Devonish
5N
Dog Kennel Hill School

The bones lay still, searching
As the snake tries and fights.

Leon Grant
5N
Dog Kennel Hill School

Living in thought of death
Thinking of souls that rest in peace
Being re-united with death
Finding life in a place where nobody seems
To care, that's the earth…
Heaven, the revolution, peace and laughter
Minds silent melody of souls in tranquillity
Placing my mind at the death of souls
The day spirit snatches me away
Learn more about life and death
Don't get twisted by evil, the devil exists
Death to come, to be and death overcome
We are all going to die, just a matter of time
Death it is.

Asanda Qumelwana
Foundation Programme Graphic Design
Cape Peninsula University of Technology
Cape Town, South Africa

Why people go to the dark side
Which has warning signs
When two Perches show you
The light side has no warning sign

Which leads you to the grave with a tombstone of a
guitar
While snakes enjoy life playing guitars
While snails enjoy living showing love to each other
While you are in a grave but see no warning dark

I speak to those who lift Black Label quarts in taverns
Those who drink from the overflowing taps of alcohol
While hijackers go for not more than one car
And gangsters use guns as their mouths for solvents

We know the price to darkness is death
We see warning signs symbolize bones of death
We still continue on to the road of darkness without
warning
We have had the warning signs to rest

Where are the preachers to show the light side?
Where are the warning signs of death?
Where are the footsteps to the light side?
I speak to those who have revealed their minds
On the light side enjoying life not death.

Fuzile Retyu
Foundation Programme Graphic Design
Cape Peninsula University of Technology
Cape Town, South Africa

They warn me
They warn me now
And again and I don't care
I thought warning

Was about scaring someone
I thought warning was about telling
Saying something just for someone
Then do, as you want

But warning is warning
You take it seriously or not
You want it or not
It will always be a warning

Xolani Hlwele
Foundation Programme Graphic Design
Cape Peninsula of University of Technology
Cape Town, South Africa

Parents were once 13,19 before coming elders
When they disagree they've got a good reason
They know what's coming up
They went to parties, clubs, had boyfriends.
What would have happened?
If it wasn't for caring parents that they had
So when saying no, there is no jealous joke,
Only to keep you safe away from harm
And avoiding doing the mistakes that they almost
spoke.

Soaps on TV are not really life
Celebrities are not always in coffee shops or parties
They have work to go to and you have your school
Fooling your parents is the same as fooling yourself
They'll be the first people you turn to, when in trouble
So why can't you listen, wait and be patient
Being wise and responsible won't hurt you
Get up and stand up for your future
Every first step always carries a second and I promise
You'll see the difference, on the third your soul will
dance
Full of joy, stand up and be proud.

Somi Longeni
Foundation Programme Graphic Design
Cape Peninsula University of Technology
Cape Town, South Africa

Barren land of love like clay
Easy bought then torn and frayed
Born forth like the morn of the day
In darkness of dismay

How this love will pass, from charm
Of arms once dearly loved.
For both the parties now involved
Fun'rals quickly do dissolve.

Anant Sharma
Exploring Creative Writing
BA Journalism

Puppeteer
Billy Mandindi

Come children gather round
Watch me act it out
with my puppet friends
Listen to my breathtaking story
read without talking
My background colours
make you sit in another world
Sit and get hypnotised
Hypnotised with happiness
A never ending story
To make it come true
My life is a story
Come and join me.

Ben Boxall
5E
Dog Kennel Hill School

The flute player
Billy Mandindi

Sun you big player,
You are big black hands
You are a stare.
You are vital breathing
With harmony flows into
The magic flute you play.
Yes, you are round and
Your broad light neck is bright
With your energy
With your breathing.
Please, Sun don't stop
to emanate your melody
I feel good.
POOOOOOOH
POOOOOOOOOOOOH
It is the sound you play!
Well done!
Sun, give me your energy
Your big hands and eyes
Where does your rhythm come?
No, don't tell me
I want to guess!
You are the nature
A ball of fire with the leaf,
The mother of everything.
You play without stop
From this infinite sky
you come to play your flute.
Do you like your task
I don't know
I don't care
reaching your daily melody
It is enough for me!
BIG ONE
POOOOOOOOOOOH.

Federico De Cicco
Moving and Tuning History
BA G.M.D. Illustration

Blow in the wind
Blow in the flute
Blow
Take in the air
Breathe in the air
Breathe, oooohhhhhh
Live life listen to the music
Blow into the flute
Dance to the music
Blow in the wind
Nothing left to lose.

Anon
BA Digital Media Production 3

I play the flute, because no one listens.
I know it's a terrible sound,
but it's the only way I can get attention.
I am terrified to be a part of the crowd,
to be one of them.
I want to be heard, seen and looked at.
I play the flute, because no one listens.

Joona Laulajainen
Exploring Creative Writing
FDA Design for Graphic Communication

Oh flute player, see your hat made of bright leaves.
How do you keep that fresh as a butterfly?
Not me, not me, my music is living and free.
Oh flute player, play something for me,
Something wild and free.
Oh flute player please, please, oh please.
Thank you, now I am truly free!
Oh flute player, see your hat made of bright leaves,
How do you keep them so fresh as a butterfly?
Not me.

Kieran Bartlett
5E
Dog Kennel Hill School

My name is Peter
I am the flute that never stop playing
I got leaves on my head
And all over is magic
I play the flute
All day I never stop until
My brother go away
I am the flute, the best in the world.

Anthony Lewin
5N
Dog Kennel Hill School

This day is for me and for you…
How often we get to listen to our heart
Feel sounds from a listener's point of view
Just as you and me when listening to this tune

This day is for me and for you…
And hearts that desire of becoming a musician
Listen can you hear my flute!
I can hear your destiny

When it is taken away
It will cause a stir of abruptness in our society
For then we will make no sound to stay
More dominant than prosperity

No no no… it won't be broken
Instead its sound awakens my soul.

Andrew Petersen
Foundation Programme Graphic Design
Cape Peninsula University of Technology
Cape Town, South Africa

A flute player playing alone
A flute player playing a tune,
A flute player in the fields,
Playing his tune with wide fingers.
A flute player playing a tune,
The sun glows yellow the sky turns blue
And one flute player is making a tune
He hears the lyrics and celebrates.

Melissa Giraldo-Ojeda
5N
Dog Kennel Hill School

The flute player lives in my village
His eyes are full of joy
I hear his music every day
Every day his music sounds different
Unique, he brings happiness
to broken hearts who hear his flute
Every day and night.
Nobody knows when he starts and stops

People in the village believe in him

Including the chief himself

They say he brings rain to dry periods

They say he brings sunshine to those in need

The flute player never speaks
He sits silent and plays his flute for people
People dance to his music
He lives in my village.

Asanda Qumelwana
Foundation Programme Graphic Design
Cape Peninsula University of Technology
Cape Town, South Africa

Turn it up; Mr. DJ
I just love this song; it's called: 'The Flute'
A-la musical
I live by the rules
With where I am going
    Still perfecting the art

I am free
Music makes me move
Bringing rhythm to my feet
And when I walk
I don't worry where the steps take me
    I flick my hands

Music unites me
Taking me places where I'm in tune
With who I am
With what I am
In a neurotic world
    I roll my shoulders

Music uplifts me
Coming from a point of touch,
Going to a point of weightlessness
The heavy soul enlightened.
Sand might drift but
    I leap through the heavens

Music flirts me
Ur eyes are enticed with the way I sway,
Ur mind tempted with fantasy
By every tangible motion
I oscillate my hips
    Music helps me

Bringing balance to harmony
Renewing an age, bringing maturity
I dance I am
Music defines me.
Listening, feeling, communicating
    Refining the silence

I invigorate my life with noise
I induce my fellow to happiness
I collaborate audio and visual stimuli
I play the flute a beat, a composition
    And have some control…

Dimitri Abels
Foundation Programme Graphic Design
Cape Peninsula University of Technology
Cape Town, South Africa

Flute players
Billy Mandindi

It is not our hands; it is not our bodies
that come to you first.
All that is background, and shadowy walls,
Organic shapes are mere decoration.
No. What is foremost,
what changes the air to meet you is music.
From wood, from mouth, from heart.
Our song.
Black and white is the world and through it
streams this tune. Listen.
Deep history, proud tradition,
To this we owe its melody
To this we owe its grace and charm
the hum of our land.

A never-ending place in harmony,
Standing before your feet,
Two flute players are we.

Kate Bellamy
Exploring Creative Writing
BA G.M.D. Illustration

A flute as gold as a coin
The coin of celebration
The celebration of the baby
The baby they are playing
Is quite cute
As the summer fruit
Floating in the air
Air as hot as the sun
The sun red as a plum
A plum tattooed by the twins
The flute of the baby
The twins with the flutes.

Anon
5N
Dog Kennel Hill School
(Spoken with an African accent)

Listen to my tune
When I blow on this stick, I have all the attention in
this room
With my special clothes that were designed for this
day
No money needs to be given to me
The joyful faces are my pay

I am the flute player
I will entertain you with my device
Mine has been especially ornamented
This will be my chance
To show these people that we are more than flute
players
We are more than famine and aids. Yes I am a flute
player
but I can be more than what's expected from my race.

Nana Opoku-Acheampong
Creative Writing
BA Media and Cultural Studies

I am the two men
That play flute
I play all day and
I play alone, my name
Is flute and his name play.
We play the same together
I am just joking
I am just a loner
I can't believe you believed me.
I play with my twin brother Peter.

Sulls Playey
5N
Dog Kennel Hill School

Two sisters playing the flute
Their mouths shaped like music
Their music is fierce
Their music is a tiger

Two sisters playing their flutes
Their mouths shaped like drummers hands
Hands shaped like dancers footprints

Two sisters playing their flutes
Jealous sisters
Playing their jealous music

Two sisters playing their flute
Playing as lovely as can be
Playing like professionals.

Adama Kamara
5E
Dog Kennel Hill School

Mother of twins
Billy Mandindi

Gather my children before I die
I have much to tell them

When I was young I dreamt of having you.
Back then, in the morning dew, I always knew

I wanted a similar life for you. Glad this did not come
to pass.
Over the years, as the hatred grew

Soweto, Soweto, we were sent to a barren home
Soweto, Soweto, where we were never Afrikaans

Your father wore a necklace of resistance around his
heart;
the phrase 'I will defy you' on his lips.

The afternoon of his disappearance I was too confused
to tell you
His body, scratched, blanched, swinging, still resonates
in my soul.

That day I felt my teats torn, unable to allow his echo
to suckle me,
much too painful, to put into… Soweto, Soweto that all
consuming hatred

Blasting the innocent far from home, God has passed
his blessing from Africa
He has allowed me to hold you once again
Stand tall and proud my most beautiful creations
But always keep a watchful eye on the storms of the
hateful.

Lee Fernandez
Creative Writing
FDA Design For Graphic Communication

Babies are a gift and a joy
But you have to be careful
It could be a naughty boy.
Girls can be a joy but
You never know they could
Be sneaking around with a boy...
If you have twins that is even
More case for you tho',
You have to wash more clothes
And wipe more bottoms
And wipe up their sick
Babies could make you switch
I wish I was still a baby but I
Could be a pain and everyone
Knows when they grow up
You could end up ashamed.

Sean Miller
5N
Dog Kennel Hill School

Dog Kennel Blues: A creative project across Boundaries and Continents.

The Image
Hard Ground Printmakers
In October 2006 the London College of Communication (LCC) held a unique exhibition entitled 'Impressions' that brought together for the first time work by the Hard Ground Printmakers, artists and print makers from South Africa. The studio was established in 1989 by Jonathan Comerford a well-known South African artist and printmaker, it was called 'Hard Ground' to reflect the difficulty independent artists experienced in gaining access to printmaking presses. The studio enabled the production of powerful socio-political images from the three decades of South African history. One section of the exhibition featured the celebrated artist/printmaker Billy Mandindi (1967–2005). All the artists were associated with the workshop where their prints and portfolios were produced. Internationally recognised, Billy became synonymous with the Hard Ground Printmakers. Kweti Nzube and Madi Phali are also portrayed in a portfolio describing the artists' view in the celebration of the last ten years of democracy in South Africa.

The Text
The idea for the exhibition developed from a partnership between LCC and Cape Peninsula University of Technology. The exhibition was the beginning of a project to develop enterprise and innovation in design and the visual arts in both institutions. The creative writing project involved LCC students working with professional writers who were engaged in running the suite of Creative Writing electives at the College. The Widening Participation team at LCC worked with

Dog Kennel Hill School pupils. In South Africa, Edwine Simon worked with students at Cape Peninsula University of Technology where they wrote poems inspired by the artists' work, many of whom were from the Cape Town area. The diversity of language and imagery provided the keys to unlocking the hidden talent of the young minds involved in this project.

Impressions
Poems and Images from Two Continents
In April 2007 an exhibition of the poems with the images was held at LCC containing the work published within this book.

London College of Communication
Undergraduate students from all four specialist Schools: Printing and Publishing, Graphic Design, Media and Creative Enterprise wrote poems in their elective programme inspired by the work of the Impressions exhibition.

Creative Writing
LCC has an established and growing community of staff and students in Creative Writing with highly popular and successful second year cross-college electives in Creative Writing, Exploring Creative Writing, Mapping the Rhythm and Writing for Design. These are delivered by established practitioners or Royal Literary Fellows attached to the College including Ronnie McGrath and Catherine Johnson. Our practice-based environment provides many opportunities for collaborative projects centred on writing text to image/creating images to text, for example Colin Jones's photographic work that inspired the Poems of Note exhibition and publication between 2004–2006.

Dog Kennel Hill School

In conjunction with the Widening Participation department at LCC, Dog Kennel Hill Primary School worked for two years with LCC on a series of printing projects. As with all previous Creative Partnerships projects at the school, the emphasis was on embedding this work in the curriculum and hence themes were drawn from relevant school topics. This returned to the themes of Creative Writing and Design within the curriculum.

The Cape Peninsula University of Technology

The establishment of the college followed more than ten years of representations by the community for the consolidation of the technical courses, which had been offered in various venues in the city. During the apartheid era, all education institutions were forced to serve a specific race group. In 1987 the Peninsula Technikon opened its doors to all South Africans. In the same year, the Cape Technikon applied for and was granted special permission to have the Government's regulation lifted on the quota for black students. Multilingualism is a great and enriching experience in the classroom. The diversity of language is a personal development for each student and was encouraged in this creative writing project where they used diversity as training on the one hand and education on the other hand. Students were invited to choose an image and write a poem in response to the image and communicate their feelings creatively in words. The students were instructed to use the image title as their poem's title. More and more the University finds these communication skills are important in an academic environment, in order to develop self-awareness, self esteem and promote healing. Students were encouraged and asked to write their poems and 'prose fragments' in their mother tongue and then translate their mother tongue poems into English.

Tony Wailey and Susana Sambade

Tony Wailey has worked within the fields of reflective practice for the last 22 years through Independent Study, Assessment of Prior Learning and Personal Development Planning. As a published novelist and poet Tony's current research focuses on Creative Learning through Creative Writing, both within the practice of creative writing as a vehicle in itself or for teaching professional development across the creative industries. Susana Sambade works as an Associate Lecturer at the College and has played a vital role in the analysis of student expectations of creative writing. She has published a number of papers on this subject.

This project would not have been possible without the work of the following people.

A big thank you to:

All Poet Contributors
Josie Barnes
Chris Bendon
Chris Bullar
Pat Bowyer
Jonathon Comerford
Colin Daniel
Caroline David
Hard Ground Printmakers
Paula Hare
Steve Higginson
Danny Hollowell
Catherine Johnson
Marisa Lea
Bill Long
Michelle Lukins
John McCarthy
Ronnie McGrath
Marilyn McMenemy
Anne Nicholls
Anthony Petrou
Susana Sambade
Andy Savery
Edwine Simon
Mary Thompson
Laura Tull
Beth Wade
Glyn Whittle

Many thanks also to the offices and Institutions below:
The Design Practice
The British Council
CLIP CETL Research, University of the Arts

Tony Wailey
Coordinator
January 2008